Recovery Leadership

Building Teams for Better Outcomes

Kenneth A. Vick
MA, CRADC, HRS, CRPR, LAC, MARS
Recovery Consulting LLC.

Dedication

To my wife, **Michelle**

Without her, I could not serve our community in the same manner. My ability to serve and lead comes from a foundation and refuge at home.

Thank you, Lord, for being the solid rock of our foundation.

Table of Contents

Recovery Definition

Recovery is a *process of change* through which individuals *improve their health and wellness*, live *self-directed* lives, and *strive to reach their full potential*.

(SAMHSA, SAMHSA's WORKING DEFINITION OF RECOVERY, 2012)

Page Blank Intentionally

Forward

This book is to help those in the behavioral health field. For many years, I have worked with community mental health agencies. I have learned that it can be one of the more toxic environments you can work in. It does not sound logical that it should harm those wanting to help others. The field is here to help people, and it does. It has been the most rewarding time in my life. But it has also been some of the most troubling times.

The expectations for programs and the lack of resources sometimes make it difficult. There is also the way leaders are promoted and grow. A clear education bias believes that degrees and licenses make leaders. Education matters, but we could look at the experience as well. I have a graduate degree in Organizational Leadership and an undergrad in Psychology. I understand the need for education. This book has information that will promote the idea that lived experience could play a more significant role in the career ladder used in behavioral health care.

I have spent years building teams that promote comfort and efficiency. Comfort means to feel good about going to work and the team you work with. Efficiency means work gets done with a "work smarter, not harder" viewpoint. Our field has significantly emphasized outcomes more than caring for each other. The teams I support and mentor move forward as leaders themselves. A good leader helps the team members grow so they can move up, even if that means they need to move on. The team is the commodity that makes a successful program. Pour into them, and they will pour into those they serve. We can do better in every part of our field. I have spent my tenure mentoring and helping others in this profession. The teams they are on are unhealthy and harm their members.

I want my experience to help others. Leadership is a privilege. I have learned to take it very seriously. Our teams can do more if our leadership is better at serving than dictating.

My past has been colorful. I am in long-term recovery from substance use disorder, depression, and PTSD. My lived and living experience helps me pay attention to how I feel. My recovery has allowed me to look at life in ways others often don't. My ability to self-assess allows me to be aware of how others may feel. Some great leaders truly help others grow. Unfortunately, more leaders do damage. I want to make a difference and help our field protect itself so it is better at helping our communities effectively.

Chapter One: Know Your Why

The behavioral health field is incredibly gratifying, as it involves the compassionate and dedicated work of assisting individuals in their journey towards better mental and emotional well-being. However, the rewards of this profession become amplified when one is part of a healthy and supportive team. In this field, the hearts of those involved are truly immense, as they possess unwavering empathy and a genuine desire to make a positive impact on the lives of others.

It is important to note that pursuing a career in behavioral health is not typically driven by financial motives, especially if one does not reach the level of a Ph.D. or doctorate through further education. Instead, individuals enter this noble calling sincerely intending to lend a helping hand to those in need. The fulfillment derived from knowing that their efforts contribute to improving another person's life forms the true essence of their professional journey. I was inspired to embark on this path with a strong desire to assist and support others. The motivation behind my original plan to enter this field stemmed from my belief in the transformative power of compassion and the potential to effect meaningful change in people's lives.

My original plan was to help the person across the desk from me. My goals were to help people get out of or avoid the lifestyle I lived for 20-plus years. I made many mistakes when I started. As I grew and learned, I discovered I wanted to help other professionals help the person across the desk. That helped me increase the number of those that I touched. Every professional I helped, I had an impact on all those they touched. I discovered the importance of leadership.

I needed to understand why I was doing what I was doing. I went from making foreman wages as a journeyman carpenter to $12.00 an hour as a counselor in training. I was a single man with a house payment, child support, college, and tithing. My spiritual beliefs fueled my drive to change professions. I believe that my calling is to serve others. All of this led to why I was changing my life path. I had to believe it was for a reason beyond myself. Years later, I know it was.

My "why" is connected to my recovery. I want to help people come out of the lifestyle I lived for over twenty years. Having lived/living experience is a massive part of my why. My life started with trauma at an early age. I didn't know what it was back then. I just thought it was normal. As I grew and learned, I discovered how many of my actions, including my substance use, were directly connected to the trauma I experienced.

This book is not about my story of recovery. But my recovery does play a role in how I grew as a leader. It is part of WHY I am writing this book. Being a servant leader is part of my leadership style. Robert Greenleaf has dramatically influenced how I serve those on our team (Greenleaf, 2020). The idea that I serve the team as a leader is challenging for many. For me, I want to help the team grow. That means I need to do what I can to make each job easier for the team. The leader's job is to serve the team, and then the team can help the participants/clients/patients— "Moving forward, I will call them clients" better.

"You don't have to have a title to be a leader on a team."

Let's get into your why. If you are reading this book, you already know why. You want to be better at leading the team you are part of. I intend to help you learn how to build on your reasons for leading. As a quick FYI, **you don't have to**

have a title to be a leader on a team. Each person should strive to be a leader on the team and in the community. The critical part of our motivation needs to be to help others. That is most likely why you are in this field. It does not mean your focus is solely on your clients. It is also for your team. The better we do at helping and lifting our co-workers, the better the quality of our daily "grind."

As a certified clinical supervisor, I have learned to coach and mentor many in this field. The Missouri Credentialing Board (MCB) certified me as a clinical supervisor early in 2014. The training made me think about how to help the team grow. I found a passion for assisting professionals to get better at helping our communities.

Your "why" needs to be understood if you want the team to grow. Simon Sinek has many books that help promote the belief of knowing your why. His book *"Find Your Why"* is a great start (Sinek, 2023).

Inspiration comes from understanding why you do what you do. Think of how your life would go when you wake up each day inspired and motivated to go to work. It has been said, "If you love your job, you never work a day in your life." I'm not sure I buy that; I love what I do. But let's face it: There are days when it's hard to find motivation. The entire point of this chapter is to help you understand why you get up each day and to help inspire your day. Some days, you may go to work because you have bills to pay. There is nothing wrong with that. But if that is the only reason to be in this profession, you will not last long. Burnout is a real thing. Plus, you don't get rich monetarily in this field. You get rich from meeting your why.

Our field is always looking to find a way to motivate our clients to make changes that will raise their quality of life. How often do you take the time to find your motivation? It is not a simple question or answer. Self-care is vital, but I'm asking about something more profound. Why are you reading this? (Thank you, by the way) If your reasoning is on bettering your life, great. If you are doing this to help improve our field and communities, even better. Your motivation and inspiration come from knowing your why.

I've always wanted to be the best I could be at everything I have ever done. Even in my past lifestyle as a criminal, I tried to be the best. US Marshals and the Federal Bureau of Prisons finally helped change that goal. Believe it or not, it was a blessing. As I grow older and continue to learn, I can see that my motivation grows as I grow. It alters direction and helps move in ways I did not foresee. It has grown from helping one person to helping the entire profession.

Leaders should feel called to help more people. I know that I am here to help our entire community/world. If you are indeed a leader, that is your calling/why as well. We tell our clients that it helps to look at a task as "I get to do …" rather than "I have to do…" – it starts to touch you on the days that you struggle. If you look at work as work, it will feel like work. I look at what I do as a blessing that I get to help others.

That helps push me through the tough days. Influential leaders are those who motivate their team members. They ensure their team is inspired to do their best work. Leaders ensure that everyone feels like they're getting what they need to be successful in the company. There are many ways to motivate people: Recognition, trust building, fostering an open environment, and keeping communication channels open are great ways to boost your team. Thinking about this can help you build a strong team that gets excited about coming to work each day. Team members do their best work when they feel motivated and inspired.

Your why is your motivation. Your motivation is what helps you walk in the door. Motivation comes from knowing your why. It is a circle. One part feeds the next. You will never be a good leader if you can't find your reason for working in this profession. A leader helps those they serve to find their 'why.' It is also the leader's job to help the team feel like they can achieve their why.

They help the entire team feel better about the daily grind. It also helps them support and care for each other. As the leader of a team, you live by example.

Motivation is a state of mind that drives us to act in a certain way. We can be motivated to get the job done and to make money. But there needs to be something else in your motivation. Teams need the feeling that it is more than just the money. **Money does not stop people from burning out.** Good leaders inspire others—it helps them feel like they're part of something bigger than themselves and encourages them to do their best work. Motivation is powerful when used correctly and can be incredibly useful.

"Money does not stop people from burning out."

You need to know some things about motivation before you can use it effectively as a leader. Understanding what motivates people at work means knowing what makes your team want to do their best work each day. People are different; some look for money, while others enjoy recognition or growth opportunities. Many in the helping professions want to help others, which is their most significant motivation, their why. Not everyone has the same motivations, so you must ask your team members how they feel and adjust accordingly based on their responses.

My recovery helped motivate me to enter this field. My past experiences helped me see that I didn't want others to struggle as I did. In my professional career, my motivation also comes from my lived experience. I have worked for really "bad" bosses and some good ones. They inspired me to write this. They inspired me to get my masters in Organizational Leadership. I do not want others in this field to live through a "bad" boss. Those bosses create an environment of drama and chaos. That will only lead to burnout and compassion fatigue. My WHY is to help change the negative feelings of burnout and compassion fatigue my colleagues experience. We are extremely short on helping professionals and cannot continue creating unhealthy work environments. We must do more to support our teams so we can do more to support our communities.

Chapter Two: Reasons for Using this Book

My experience in this field has shown me a great need for more leadership skills. Stress and expectations connect to every part of the helping profession. We put so much effort into helping others that we sometimes forget to care for ourselves and our team. The team is the most valuable commodity in a program. Caring for your team is the foundation for building a good program and healthy work environment. This chapter looks at some of my history in the field and the things I've discovered as I've built healthy teams.

"The team is the most valuable commodity in a program."

In chapter one, we discussed why we do this. It is foundational to understanding why our teams work so hard to help other people. My why comes from working on teams and for leaders who were not overly healthy. That's not to say they were terrible leaders, but they did not promote a culture of care and support within the team. I have been on the edge of burnout and felt I did not want to go to work because of the work culture. It was not because of the clients we serve but because of the programs I worked in. Leadership in those programs created a culture of fear. It always felt like it was us against them. Being siloed or segregated in our programs added to the negative feelings. It felt like it was case managers against counselors, and they all looked down on peer specialists and monitors.

We expect our clients to struggle, have bad days, and act in ways that may be frustrating. That is why they come to see us. It's the programs and the leaders that burn us out. Leaders do not create separation in a team in healthy programs. We can be better.

Early in my career, I asked many questions. I always wanted to know why we were doing this paperwork and logging that information. At that time, I had a boss, **Kent**

Jewell, who answered my questions and helped me understand why we had to do what we were doing. It was an old-school approach, but I could understand it. I learned what documentation went with what billing source, which helped me understand the reasoning behind so much paperwork.

At that time, I did not know we were duplicating work because of poor record-keeping software. **A good leader tries to supply the team with the right tools for the job.** Finding the right tool makes the job easier and less stressful. As you can see, I am a person who always wants to know why. Understanding the why helps drive me to continue to move forward and help as best I can.

"A good leader tries to supply the team with the right tools for the job."

My career has had bosses/leaders who helped me along the way. Each time I moved to a new company, I could ask my questions and understand the why of what we were doing. Most of what I learned was dissatisfaction rather than satisfaction with the company's reasoning. Please do not get this wrong. I worked for companies that did a lot of good for people and our community. However, they did not do well for the team, resulting in a rollover of employees. I say employees here instead of team members because those companies treated people as employees, not team members.

You may also notice that I use the phrase 'boss,' meaning someone who dictates rather than inspires. I look back on them as a blessing because I learned from each one, positives and negatives. I am the leader I am today because of those experiences. Following some of my ideas in this book will help reduce turnover in your workforce. Our field is struggling to fill positions. The future will worsen if we don't consider how we support our teams.

Being in recovery from PTSD and substance use disorder helped me understand the client side of a program. As a client, I experienced a correctional way of trying to make a change. My counseling experience started in the 1980s, and the beliefs were archaic. If punishment worked, our prisons would be more successful. I did find recovery on my "federal vacation," but that was not close to the first time I served a sentence. Treatment in the past was not strength-based and focused on the negatives, leading to negative feelings. Again, my experience and history taught me what kind of counselor I wanted to be.

I knew I did not want to make the people I served feel the way programs made me feel. It is the same thing with leadership. I did not want to be a leader who made those on the team feel like employees. I wanted them to feel like team members. Team means every person has value; titles are simply titles, and every person on the team is precious. That is the feeling that I wanted every team I led to feel. They were valuable, and I wanted them to know it. **A person who feels valued does more. A person who feels important will serve better.** It is hard to motivate clients when your team isn't motivated. Compassion fatigue doesn't just make it difficult to feel empathy for your clients, but it also affects your feelings for your team.

One component of compassion fatigue is burnout, which is associated with too much work and insufficient resources to do that work well. The resource needed is also time for self-care and feeling valued. Burnout can result in depression and anxiety, physical and emotional exhaustion, less enjoyment of work, and poor outcomes. Our job as leaders is to help our team avoid these issues.

"A person who feels valued does more."
"A person who feels important will serve better."

There's a workforce shortage in our field that we all feel deeply, which adds to stress and burnout. Over the years, I have built relationships with team members that have lasted beyond time at a company. Team members from programs in my past tend to join me at new programs because of the culture WE created. I say we here because I did not make these teams and the culture. My job was to bring in team members who supported each other. The team members create the culture; because of this, our clients and communities get the rewards. The team's reward is the ability to come to work each day, feel valued, feel heard, and look forward to coming to work. I have always been able to keep an entire team or close to it because of the culture created.

Many companies look at how they can keep their employees or staff full, but they don't look closely enough at how their employees feel about walking in the door. They tend to think money is the main factor in work satisfaction, and it's not in this field. I use the wording staff and employees here as an example of how many programs look at the people who work for them. Just like the trauma-informed care language we use as professionals, we should use the same thought in the language we use for our team.

When a team member feels like a team member rather than an employee, it adds to their inspiration and motivation. A motivated and inspired team member adds depth and quality to the services provided to the community. Many memes state, "People don't leave jobs; they leave bad leadership." If your leadership style does not promote health and wellness within the team, then I hope the rest of this book can help.

Real leaders understand the impact of unhealthy cultures on people and organizational success. They recognize that individuals are likely to leave when they feel unsatisfied mentally and emotionally. These leaders prioritize creating a foundation for a culture that meets basic needs and provides a sense of fulfillment and emotional reward. They cultivate an environment where employees feel valued, supported, and inspired to excel. These leaders aim to establish a culture that brings out the best in people by fostering positive relationships, encouraging open communication, and promoting personal growth. This commitment to building a healthy and nurturing work environment sets real leaders apart, enabling them to attract and retain talented individuals dedicated to the organization's success.

Chapter Three: How to Make Good Organizations Better

In this chapter, I'll talk about making a good organization better.

Making a good organization better means I respect programs that help people. Bad organizations do not last very long in the behavioral health field. Bad leadership and cultures may have negative impacts, but the program services may have value. If you work for an organization you consider a poorly run organization, this chapter will be of assistance. I mainly say 'making good organizations better' because all programs have strengths and positives. Our world has enough negativity. I don't need to add to it. I want this to inspire and lift.

It would help if you started with what the mission of the program you're working with is trying to achieve. Behavioral health programs improve life quality and build better communities in a perfect world. You can begin developing a plan after examining the mission and seeing if the work fits the task. It is also essential to look at a vision statement to see if the vision for the future includes the mission. Once you have discovered how well your beliefs and skills match the mission statement, you can better understand the plan to build growth and stability.

I have worked in many programs with great mission and vision statements. I also know the work focused on business outcomes rather than the quality of life outcomes for the community served. That did not make those harmful programs. It made them misguided regarding what they started trying to accomplish initially. Being misguided can cause confusion and discord in a program. You might re-evaluate your goals and motivation if you do not align with the program's mission and vision. With time and shifts in leadership, goals and missions can change.

Changes that pull your program away from its original mission can be hard to correct. Programs change when looking at the day-to-day work and how we truly achieve our goals. So, the first part is ensuring that your personal goals and the mission and vision statements align. It is hard to work in a program that does not align with your personal beliefs. Make sure you understand how the purpose of the program fits your purpose.

Once you have discovered how well the goals for yourself as a leader and the program in general line up, you can start looking at the team you have that supports these things. I do not recommend that you start looking directly at the program regarding changing clinical goals, styles, and modalities too quickly. Focusing on the team and the people truly doing the work is much more critical. It takes time to evaluate and get to know and understand the team in the program and what drives them to do what they do each day.

In the past, I have invested significant amounts of time and effort into delving deeply into understanding the dynamics of a team and how effectively its members collaborate. This process, admittedly, has often taken several months to accomplish. Over time, I have been able to discern which members genuinely care about and actively support the team's overall well-being. I have also identified those who do not exhibit these qualities.

It is crucial to grasp that initial perceptions and observations about a team should be cautiously approached.

They may be a harmful or toxic work culture that fosters a sense of resignation among its members. However, I have observed instances where individual staff members adopted a healthier attitude once their surroundings transformed positively. They were then able to blossom into extraordinary team contributors. In other words, a shift in organizational culture towards a more positive and nurturing direction can lead to remarkable personal growth and development among team members.

You can have many brilliant, intelligent team members like counselors, peer specialists, case managers, monitors, and more who are different parts of the team. Being bright and good at your job is not all there is to be a good team member. I have met many extremely good people who do their jobs well in terms of tasks related to their positions. I have also seen what happens when good people focus on a team rather than individual tasks. If a team member only focuses on doing what fits for their position, you will see less teamwork. Less teamwork creates less satisfaction and poor outcomes.

The behavioral health field is difficult and stressful, especially when you don't have team members to lean on. We all do and feel better when we can rely on our teammates.

Having a good attitude is essential, and you can teach skills. I have looked at resumes many times to find skills. I can teach skills that may be lacking. It is easier to teach skills than attitude. I focus on discovering the team members' attitudes and how well they want their team members to succeed. One straightforward thing I think is essential to look for is someone who says, "That is not in my job description." It shows a poor attitude and little willingness to be part of a team. I do not keep people that think like that long on a team. It will erode the supportive nature and culture of a good team.

Those who want to focus only on what they consider part of their job description are often more self-serving than team-serving. **It's essential to have people who want to serve each other as much as the clients or community.** The teams I've been a part of have helped build and lift each other consistently and support each other in good and bad times.

I would say that the team is foundational in helping programs improve. People pulling together can make a massive difference in the community. One person unwilling to pull together can significantly increase the struggle of those who do pull together.

"It's essential to have people who want to serve each other as much as the clients or community."

It is essential not to make rash decisions with a team that has been together for a while. My experience has shown me that what appears on the surface may not be what is real. The people who want to be motivated within a team may have turned quiet. With a quiet team member, getting to know them and what drives them takes longer. Poor culture makes people quiet. I believe in "addition by subtraction," but I warn against subtracting people off the team without time to understand the internal drive of that person. The culture of some programs can make a person afraid to open up. When the culture creates a feeling of every person for themselves, it takes time to see who truly wants to be part of a team.

The behavioral health field is full of cultural competence training. I prefer to call it cultural humility rather than competence. I'm humble enough to know I don't know. These trainings focus on the people and community served. They tend to focus on clients rather than the team. To help programs, we need to focus on the culture within the program within the team doing the work. If you want a better program, you must build or support a culture of care and understanding within the team.

When it comes down to it, the way to make an organization better is to build a culture that supports each other, and it starts from the top. I consider everyone on the team a leader and a valuable team member. However, most of the weight for creating and maintaining a culture comes from the top, such as directors and supervisors. The most dangerous thing I have witnessed and been a part of is a poor culture within the behavioral health field. **Pay may attract people, but cultures keep them.** To make the program you are working in better, ensure you have a culture of care and support.

"Pay may attract people, but cultures keep them."

Chapter Four: Leadership Skills

Leadership skills that I've learned come from a multitude of experiences. I've spent years learning from my mistakes and witnessing the good, bad, and ugly of other leaders. Claremont Lincoln University (CLU) and its graduate program for organizational leadership with a concentration on ethics is another way I've learned leadership. (Claremont Lincoln University, 2023) My time with Claremont was a blessing to help me learn better communication styles and understand specific techniques.

CLU's Master of Arts in Organizational Leadership program prepared me to lead diverse organizations toward positive social change.

I chose a concentration in Ethics. I learned more about navigating diversity, thinking critically, managing complexity, and meeting strategic goals within an ethical context. My formal education changed how I look outside my personal experiences. It helped me look at my lived experiences and add critical thinking and evaluation for better understanding.

Much of my learning comes from experience. I spent a considerable number of years as a foreman on a carpentry crew before moving to the helping professions. Leadership styles are very different for construction workers. I expand a bit more on this topic later in this book. In the helping professions, I've been able to witness and experience leaders who had many different styles that could help or hurt, or both. In my opinion, most leaders in our world help and hurt. The intention may be to help, but the lack of understanding and empathy causes errors in the intended results. Bosses, not leaders, know they hurt people but only care about the bottom line.

As a clinician, I learned to pay attention to feelings, emotions, and how people feel after interactions. The feelings I brought from interactions with past leaders influence my leadership styles today. How my team members feel after interacting with me is essential. I want the team to feel good, perform well, and find satisfaction with their work.

Servant leadership is a style that I've grown fond of, along with authentic leadership. As a servant leader, I make the team's job easier. A servant leader helps remove barriers that make it harder for a team to excel. An authentic leader is open with the team, and shares struggles and strengths openly as part of the team. Being authentic allows the team to get to know you without hiding behind a facade. Both leadership styles complement each other and are assets in my ability to lead others.

Authentic leadership is about being honest and genuine. An authentic leader can inspire loyalty and trust in the team by consistently displaying who they are as a person. It helps the team know how you feel about them and their performance. Common characteristics help identify those with these skills. Below is a list of skills/styles of an authentic leader.

1. Purpose and vision: Authentic leaders rely on purpose and vision to achieve long-term goals. They're not easily distracted from helping the team toward those goals. They look at the big picture, avoiding letting little things get in the way. Authentic leaders can also share that vision with their team to inspire them toward common goals and purposes.

2. Self-discipline: Self-discipline helps the leader be an example of how to reach goals without distraction and adds consistency to the team. Staying focused and structured with tasks is easier for the team if they see the leader as an example. A disciplined leader helps the team know what to expect. If the leader has discipline, the team will know that there are similar expectations for them.

3. Core Values: Authentic leaders know who they are and are confident in their beliefs. A robust set of core values shows that they are unwilling to compromise values to get ahead. They also help their team hold to similar standards. Leaders can be flexible and open to new ways of doing things while still holding to their values. Core values are the principles that guide a person's actions. They represent the foundational beliefs that help an individual navigate complex situations. It helps them keep their identity and culture at the forefront.

4. Empathy: Authentic leaders focus on empathy because they lead with the heart. Being aware of their team's needs and the team's feelings helps to support them. Authentic leaders show their heart and passion.

Empathy comes from understanding the feelings and viewpoints of others. It comes from putting effort into seeing things from the other's point of view. It's the ability to understand the team member's thoughts and feelings about a situation from their viewpoint rather than your own. It differs from sympathy, where the thoughts and feelings of another move one, but they maintain an emotional distance.

5. Self-awareness: Leaders have to be able to do self-assessments themselves. Authentic leaders have a strong sense of self. Self-assessment helps leaders learn from their choices and build skills for the future. SAMHSA states the importance of self-assessment in their TAP 21 Addiction Counseling Competencies— 120 and 123. (SAMHSA, TAP 21 Addiction Counseling Competencies, 2017) A leader needs to know their strengths and weaknesses to maximize their effects. They learn from their mentors so they can continue to grow. They identify their mistakes and strive to avoid repeating them. Authentic leaders typically set personal development goals that help them improve their work/life balance.

6. Transparent: Authentic leaders are open and honest. Transparency is a crucial characteristic of an authentic leader. Good leaders understand that transparency sets a foundation of trust. It helps encourage team members to be transparent with the leader. Being transparent as a team opens doors for better communication. Transparent communication is both good and bad information openly shared, allowing the team to see the why behind the words. The benefits of being transparent are increased collaboration, enhanced trust, and increased innovation. An open leader also promotes the feeling that the team can be open.

7. Give Credit: Authentic leaders prioritize their team's success over personal recognition. They understand that individual achievements are crucial in a collective effort, and thus, they ensure that credit goes where it is due. By acknowledging the contributions of team members, authentic leaders not only boost their confidence but also foster a strong sense of camaraderie and synergy within the team. However, it is essential to note that while some leaders excel at sharing credit with their team members, there are instances where they might inadvertently neglect acknowledging their role in the success of a project. Acknowledging one's contributions is equally essential, as it empowers leaders to continue leading effectively and sets an example for others to do the same. Striking a balance between recognizing individual efforts and acknowledging personal involvement is a characteristic of authentic leadership. It demonstrates humility, fairness, and the ability to motivate and inspire the team to achieve more success collectively.

8. Open-minded: An authentic leader knows there is more than one way to complete a task. They are open to different ideas and points of view. They listen to understand the way the team sees the possibilities. The authentic leader knows that being open to more options and ideas will only add to the possible outcomes. Being open-minded involves being receptive to various ideas, arguments, and information. Being open-minded is generally considered a positive quality. It is necessary when thinking critically and rationally. An open-minded approach will involve asking questions and actively searching for information that challenges your beliefs. It promotes the belief that others can express their beliefs even if their viewpoints differ.

Servant Leaders start as servants first and then grow into leaders. That leader is very different from one who is a leader first. The leader-first and the servant-first are two different types. A servant-leader focuses on the growth of people and the communities to which they belong. Traditional leadership typically involves the accumulation of and the exercise of power. Servant-leaders share power and put the needs of others first so they can help people develop and perform at high standards. Robert Greenleaf states, "The difference manifests itself in the care taken by the servant-first to make sure that other people's highest priority needs are being served." (Greenleaf, 2020)

Skills in this style of leadership are:

1. Do those served grow? Servant leaders help build other leaders. Leadership assessments of qualities show in the team and its members' growth. The goal is growth for each team member and maybe even moving on to a leadership role elsewhere. You can also see the effect on the least privileged in society. Do they benefit, or are they deprived? A servant leader demonstrates care for others and helps the team and community meet goals and grow.

2. Ethical Character: A servant leader is someone who maintains integrity. They will make decisions based on ethics and values and display humility. The authentic leader and servant leader are the same in this area. Ethical leaders continue to study and grow to stay ethical and faithful to their beliefs even when there are grey areas in situations.

3. Person-Centered: A servant leader meets the team/team members where they are but does not leave them there. They strive to help each person grow to the goals set by each team/team member. A servant leader puts focus on the individual and helps them grow. They have a community vision as they help. Helping one person but harming the community does not align. The skill and knowledge to balance between the person and the community are vital. The idea is that each of us can find solutions for ourselves and have the ability to make appropriate choices. Leaders benefit from learning more motivational interviewing technics to stay person-centered.

4. Skilled at Communicating: Communication skills are crucial in every leadership style, serving as a cornerstone for effective and successful leaders. Servant leadership distinguishes itself among these styles by emphasizing being an exceptional listener. By actively engaging in the art of listening, the servant leader fosters an atmosphere that encourages open communication and feedback from their team members. Such a skill promotes a deeper understanding of diverse perspectives and concerns within the team and builds trust and rapport, creating an environment conducive to growth and collaboration. Additionally, effective listening empowers the servant leader to make informed decisions, ensuring that the needs and aspirations of their team are included. The servant leader's dedication to mastering communication through active listening sets them apart and enables them to cultivate interpersonal relationships while driving organizational success.

5. Relationship Builder: Servant leaders dedicate energy to continuously enhancing and deepening the relationships within their teams. They strongly emphasize fostering diversity, promoting equity, and ensuring inclusion at all levels. Servant leaders create an environment that values and respects every team member's unique perspectives and backgrounds by working toward these goals. One of the critical ways servant leaders foster strong relationships is by leveraging and building upon the strengths of their teams. Rather than fixating on weaknesses or shortcomings, they recognize and amplify the talents and abilities that each individual brings to the table.

It increases overall team productivity and cultivates a sense of confidence and self-assurance among team members. In addition to emphasizing strengths, servant leaders also play a crucial role in navigating conflicts within the team. They possess the necessary skills and insight to deftly manage disagreements or tensions that may arise, ensuring conflicts get resolved fairly and constructively.

When managing effectively, these leaders understand that conflict can lead to greater understanding and stronger relationships within the team. Servant leaders are committed to continuously improving their teams' overall dynamics and effectiveness. By prioritizing relationship-building, supporting diversity, promoting equity, and fostering inclusion, they create an environment where individuals feel valued, heard, and empowered to contribute their best. Through their efforts, servant leaders cultivate a team that is united, resilient, and driven toward collective success.

Servant leaders need to understand the possibilities in the future so they can anticipate things that may impact the organization/community. A strong vision for your team and program will help support and build stronger communities. The servant leader can establish trust and confidence with your team. They set quality standards and delegate responsibilities to promote growth. Creating a culture that promotes openness and accountability is the goal of a servant leader.

"I never wanted to be a boss, but I wanted to make a difference."

A truly effective leader uses the skills in this chapter to build teams and communities that support progress. Coaching a team will add to the growth of a community. Your leadership skills are foundational in this area. In my years as a leader, I have grown to build more skills as an authentic and servant leader. My first drive was to serve those in our community and help improve the quality of life. As I learned and grew, I understood that I could significantly impact more people as I grew as an effective leader. **I never wanted to be a boss, but I wanted to make a difference.** Making a difference is precisely what good leaders do. Poor leaders are toxic and focus on being the boss, setting the plan and the rules, and dictating authority.

Many leaders in the behavioral health field are made leaders without the skills to lead people. They may be able to lead programs, but it takes people to make successful programs. A real leader can lead people and programs for the betterment of all. As a successful leader, I have focused on building other leaders so they can move on and support our community and programs.

Chapter Five: Team Building

I have had many people in my career tell me to write a book about how to build a team. I am blessed to have the ability to bring people together to build teams that support programs and our community. My professional career in the behavioral health arena consists of rebuilding multiple programs. Rebuilding a program does not necessarily mean the program itself was terrible. Many of the programs had good standards and qualities. Good qualities in a program have little to no meaning if the team promoting those qualities struggles. The best program in the world will underperform when the team is not cohesive and supportive of each other. This chapter will discuss what I have learned in building teams over the years.

One of the first things you need to do is identify the type of leader you are. Great teams with poor leaders will have little to no success. The first thing I had to do when I started working to build teams was start working on myself as a leader. The prior chapter gives many ideas about how I started working on myself. Everything in Chapter 4 is something I identified as things needed in me as a leader. I could discuss toxic leadership and point out leaders' lack of skills. **I would rather focus on strengths than attack the negative.** We have all seen and been a part of programs with toxic leadership.

You can allow your experience with those leaders to form the type of leader you want to be now. I do not look down on the poor leadership I have been subjected to. Those leaders gave me experience so I could grow as a leader myself. They were beneficial to me in the communities I serve.

"I would rather focus on strengths than attack the negative."

A few exceptional leaders who played a significant role in my past shaped and cultivated certain qualities within me that have become the bedrock of my leadership and continue to influence me today. Through their guidance and trust, I had the freedom to harness my unique visionary abilities, thereby contributing to growth and progress. These leaders have become invaluable mentors, still assisting me in discerning and refining my thoughts, impulses, and motivations.

Their impact remains undeniable, constantly reminding me of the importance of mentorship in our lives. Even in the highest echelons of leadership, such as the executive director, it is crucial to have someone trustworthy to offer an unbiased perspective and prevent hasty decisions driven by emotions, which could potentially lead to adverse consequences.

"If you genuinely want a quality team, allow the team to be part of the hiring process."

The hiring process is vital when you're looking at building a team. I have told many an applicant that I know they have the skills and abilities to do the job because I've looked at their resume. A common statement I use is I know you can do the job, but can you fit the team, that is what this interview is about. I firmly believe that interviews should be more than just me as the leader in the applicant. For numerous years, I've had multiple members of the team join an interview so I can get feedback from other points of view.

It only makes sense to allow the team to be part of the hiring decisions. The new hire will work with the team, and I may miss some nuances that others catch. **If you genuinely want a quality team, allow the team to be part of the hiring process.**

I ask a few simple questions during interviews to gauge the type of person I speak with. I always ask what kind of supervision they feel best fits their personality. Understanding the kind of supervision a person thinks they thrive under helps me understand how best to support the individual if they become part of the team. Many applicants look for good communication and support without micromanaging. I will also ask the team that is part of the interview to share a bit about what they feel works in supervision. Asking what an applicant looks for in a team member is another question I think is essential. I also asked what they think a quality team looks like. When you understand someone else's view of a good team, you have a better chance of meeting that individual where they are. The entire point of these questions is to discover if this individual fits the team.

Too often, interviews assess whether an individual possesses the necessary capabilities to fulfill the job requirements. However, it is essential to recognize that the information provided by a resume should already provide a foundational understanding of the candidate's qualifications. While it is undoubtedly essential to inquire about their proficiency in computer skills and the ability to take accurate notes in a timely manner, as well as other fundamental aspects, it is equally crucial to go beyond these basics. During the interview process, I delve deeper into the candidate's approach to utilizing various modalities in providing services. Furthermore, I also explored their perception of their strengths and how they believe these assets can contribute to their effectiveness in the role.

Nevertheless, the overarching focus of the interview revolved around the concept of teamwork. By emphasizing teamwork, the intention is to gauge the candidate's ability to collaborate effectively within a group dynamic. It not only highlights their interpersonal skills and capacity to communicate with others but also provides insight into their adaptability, flexibility, and willingness to contribute to a collective effort.

Ultimately, a successful candidate must possess not only the requisite skills and expertise but also the ability to integrate into the existing team structure. By broadening the interview scope beyond the traditional assessment of qualifications, we can better understand the candidate's potential for success.

One of the last questions I always ask is, "If I made you an offer, when could you start?" It is an area that will show the character of the person you are interviewing, just a tiny part. It is relatively simple and obvious to say that if someone has a job and says they can start immediately, their character may not fit the teams I build. Even if they are leaving a horrible situation, you should always give notice.

"A Leader's job is to inspire their team more than direct them."

There's more to building teams than the hiring process. Teams become stronger with good leadership. An outstanding leader puts effort into knowing each team member and understanding their goals and strengths. If you cannot focus on each team member's strengths or goals for the future, you are missing part of that person. When you value the goals of somebody on your team, that helps motivate and inspire them. **A leader's job is to inspire their team more than direct them.**

Through extensive experience in my career, encompassing various highs and lows alike, I have come to understand the importance of emphasizing the team while concurrently recognizing the value of each individual. Regarding achieving optimal program success, I firmly believe in prioritizing the team's collective efforts. However, to attain a holistic and all-encompassing triumph, it is equally imperative to delve into the intricacies of each team member's unique strengths, weaknesses, and personal aspirations.

This comprehensive approach facilitates the creation of an environment where every individual feels acknowledged, respected, and supported in their endeavors. Consequently, the unity within the team fosters an atmosphere conducive to growth and accomplishment toward the desired objectives, thus leading to ultimate success.

You cannot be a good leader without inspiring others to lead in their way. My goal in team building is straightforward: to help others succeed. I believe everyone can be a leader in one form or another. That does not mean that everybody can be a behavioral health leader or know how to be a part of a good team. I believe that everyone can be an example in various ways. My belief allows me to help people grow and reach the goals they have for their personal and professional lives. As a leader, I expect the people on my team to move on to different companies and continue to grow and support the community. I would love to find a way to keep everyone on my team so that they can continue to raise their pay and give them the promotions and recognition they deserve. Unfortunately, that is not how life works. You can only have so many leaders with titles on the team.

I support people moving on to bigger and better things. I help them build stronger resumes that will support them and their families in the future. I see it as a win-win because when people move on, they take some skills and team feelings they gained on our team to the next company. It works like ripples on the top of the water from a stone thrown. The ripples of that individual moving to another company and adding some of the knowledge they've gained to help build a team at a different program help our entire community.

The fear of training my replacement has never plagued me. The idea of someone coming in and seamlessly stepping into my role does not fill me with apprehension or concern.

On the contrary, I approach this concept with unwavering confidence and a steadfast belief in my capabilities. As long as I diligently and wholeheartedly perform my duties to the best of my ability, there is no cause for worry. I believe hiring bright and intelligent individuals should not evoke any dread in me. Instead, it is an opportunity for mutual growth and shared knowledge.

When I surround myself with such talent, it helps continuous learning and personal development. The presence of these exceptional individuals adds value not only to the organization but also to my professional journey. **You have built your team poorly if you are the most intelligent person on your team.** I can expand my skillset alongside these brilliant minds by fostering an environment that encourages collaboration and open-mindedness.

Together, we create a synergistic effect that propels us forward toward success. Embracing the possibility of training my replacement offers me the chance to broaden my horizons, refine my abilities, and focus on self-improvement. With this mindset, I approach each day with excitement and enthusiasm, confident that the prospects of more extraordinary achievements lie ahead. The fear of being surpassed ceases when I perceive it as an opportunity to expand my knowledge, hone my skills, and cultivate relationships with extraordinary individuals who share my passion for growth and excellence.

"You have built your team poorly if you are the most intelligent person on your team."

Chapter Six: Training Peer Specialists and How to use those with lived experience

There have been numerous noteworthy transformations and advancements within the behavioral health field throughout the past two decades. A critical aspect that has emerged as pivotal in the recovery process is the recognition and significance of lived and living experiences. However, despite these advancements, overcoming prevailing prejudices, education bias, and misconceptions associated with individuals in recovery remains imperative. Additionally, we must grasp the essence of the definition of recovery, acknowledging that it is not merely a static endpoint but rather an ongoing journey of self-discovery and growth.

"Recovery is a process of change through which individuals improve their health and wellness, live self-directed lives, and strive to reach their full potential."

(SAMHSA, SAMHSA's WORKING DEFINITION OF RECOVERY, 2012)

The power of a peer is impressive when you see how they open doors and break down communication walls. When a clinical team learns how to utilize a person with lived and living experience, it strengthens their ability to serve people struggling with their behavioral health. I've spent years helping teams understand the proper use of a peer specialist. For countless years, I've seen supervisors struggle with best practices when it comes to peer specialists. The peer specialist is a unique role newer to our field and still incredibly misunderstood. **A peer specialist is not a case manager, counselor, mentor, or sponsor.** A peer's power comes from sharing parts of their story in recovery and helping people see the benefits of each point of progress. It helps clients see that they have someone who understands and has been through similar struggles.

"A peer specialist is not a case manager, counselor, mentor, or sponsor."

Certified Peer Specialists (CPS) titles may differ from state to state. You can call them recovery coaches, peer support, or whatever title fits and works within your state. For ease of writing, I will use CPS moving forward. A CPS's primary meaning is a person recovering from a behavioral health issue. A person with lived and living experience and is on a recovery pathway. The phrase lived, and living experience is essential for multiple reasons. It is essential to acknowledge that an individual may effectively manage a substance use disorder as it lies in remission(Lived) while concurrently navigating the complexities of a bipolar diagnosis(Living). It can be comprehended through the lens of the stages of change, meaning that the substance use disorder has transitioned into the maintenance stage, wherein the individual is diligently working towards sustained progress. At the same time, bipolar disorder, requiring active intervention and management, resides within the action stage, demanding constant attention and proactive measures. This intricate mix of these two influential factors shows the nature of personal experiences and underscores the process of self-improvement and growth. CPSs have a solid understanding of lived and living experiences, which opens doors that can create a sense of safety.

CPS trains with an emphasis on meeting those served where they are. Much of the training fits well with a harm reduction model. It keeps a focus on being person-centered rather than program-centered. After years of training certified peers to serve our communities, I have seen how harm reduction principles fit exceptionally well. It is a peer specialist's job to help the individual they are working with meet goals that the individual sets for themselves. Clinical programs have claimed this style of person-centered treatment planning as foundational for years. But, a peer specialist is specifically trained to meet the individual they are working with to meet their recovery goals, not the program's treatment goals. The CPS has an understanding of treatment goals and supports the team. But they also spend time simply on recovery goals each individual has.

"Feeling heard and understood is priceless regarding safety and reducing harm to those we serve."

The power of a CPS is impressive. When clients walk through your door at possibly one of the lowest points in their life, they're vulnerable. The ability to activate a trauma response is very high in a client's recovery process. Talking to someone who has lived a similar experience can lower stress and anxiety—lowered stress and anxiety results in more than just the person you serve feeling safer. It also impacts how well this individual will work with the rest of the team. Helping the client feel like they are understood is essential, which is a crucial role for a CPS. **Feeling heard and understood is priceless regarding safety and reducing harm to those we serve.** A CPS can help make improvements in many programs. They are showing what recovery looks like. It helps the team see that recovery can happen. The CPS can also share what helped and hurt when they went through similar services. Knowledge is power.

Issues with using a CPS on a team tend to be connected directly to supervision. Supervisors in a behavioral health program need more training to work with a CPS. It is not uncommon for supervisors or bosses to possess an overarching belief in their expertise, assuming they understand how programs work. Consequently, they expect everyone to conform and acclimate to their predefined notion of how programs function. Many of these beliefs come from the formal education received by the supervisor. Unfortunately, most formal educators do not know how to use or what a CPS does. Trying to get past all the education biases created by our institutes of "higher" learning can be very taxing.

Another issue is the stigma connected with those in recovery. People on your team still need to be more open about what recovery looks like, even when connected to a certified professional. If a team member is biased towards a CPS and does not understand what recovery looks like, the odds are that they will also have a lower opinion of the clients they serve. Over the years, I have seen too many professionals look down on the people they serve. There's a definite need for more education regarding peer specialists, recovery definitions, and harm reduction.

Our profession has gotten better at understanding the importance of peer specialists. Over the last ten years, we have started to use peer specialists in clinical programs with incredible results. Certified peer specialists can open doors that clinical team members can't. A harm reduction framework and certified peer training are incredibly similar. A trained peer specialist can significantly impact stigma and help increase the feeling of safety to the people we serve. **Peer specialists are living blueprints of what recovery looks like.** The blueprint helps clients and the clinical team see and gain understanding.

"Peer specialists are living blueprints of what recovery looks like."

Every clinician has had clients that they couldn't reach. The clinician may be exceptionally well trained and good at what they do. No matter how well some clinicians communicate, there will still be limitations in the ability to open doors with some they serve. A good clinician knows when to pull a certified peer specialist into a session. I supervised a team with a licensed counselor and a CPS that functioned together like coffee and mornings. Between myself as the supervisor and them in their roles, we made a trio that helped clients make considerable strides in their recovery. Peer specialists can open a door because of their lived experience and how they trained to become a CPS. Clinicians have more rigid rules, modalities, and directions to follow than a CPS does.

A CPS has a code of ethics and follows guidelines, slightly different from clinical ethical codes. A peer specialist can be more open and share how they moved through a similar struggle. Sharing this lived experience in a session with the client is something a counselor can't do in the same fashion. A supervisor's job is to help the clinician and the CPS learn to function together to benefit those they serve. If the clinician or supervisor has no idea how to utilize a CPS, the team will continue to spin their wheels and struggle. That same struggle becomes connected/transferred to the quality of care the client is getting. A well-trained peer specialist is kind of like an interpreter. The CPS can facilitate communication between the clinical team and the client. **Better communication creates a better feeling of safety and more progress for the client**. Clinicians will agree that better communication would solve many of their struggles in counseling sessions.

"Better communication creates a better feeling of safety and more progress for the client."

Hiring a CPS takes skill and understanding. A CPS is not the same as hiring a clinician. With a clinician, you can look at a school transcript and gain an understanding of their abilities. Hiring a CPS is about learning the recovery of the CPS and the attitude along with communication skills they have learned in their recovery. CPSs have mass amounts of passion, so you also want to find out how well they can reign in their passion and stay ethical in their services. Take the time to get to know them and help them feel comfortable like you would with the client. It will help you get more insight into their world and what they can share with the clients in your program. **The power of a peer is immense when coupled with good supervision.** Many issues encountered with peer specialists are tracked directly back to the quality of supervision they have received. As the supervisor, you are responsible for building that relationship to best utilize peers' skills in the workplace.

"The power of a peer is immense when coupled with good supervision."

Chapter Seven: Recovery-Oriented Systems of Care

Recovery Oriented Systems of Care (ROSC) are health and human service organizations that inspire hope for recovery. A ROSC supports the idea that there are many pathways to recovery. Recovery-oriented activities include traditional treatment services and alternative therapies, including peer recovery coaching, acupuncture, meditation, music, art therapy, and many more. A ROSC focuses on connecting a system of care with the resources in a community. Many community programs partner with other disciplines like housing, food insecurities, mental health, and primary care. A ROSC contains a variety of individualized, person-centered, and strength-based services. A healthy ROSC provides individuals and families with more options to make better decisions regarding services. Services are easy to navigate and feel welcoming. The fundamentals of a ROSC is the involvement of people in recovery and their families. It takes the entire community to improve access and service quality. Many of our communities are siloed and don't communicate as well. **A healthy community works together for the betterment of all.**

"A healthy community works together for the betterment of all."

Recovery manifests itself in many ways, each unique to the individual experiencing it. There is no one-size-fits-all approach to overcoming personal challenges and finding healing. In light of this, the concept of a Recovery-Oriented System of Care (ROSC) aims to provide diverse options and opportunities for individuals to navigate their recovery journey and move forward in life. ROSC recognizes that what may work for one person may not necessarily work for another and thus encourages a personalized and holistic approach to supporting individuals on their path to wellness. By offering an array of resources, services, and support systems, ROSC seeks to create an environment where individuals can access the specific tools and strategies that resonate with them, empowering them to reclaim their lives and pave their unique path toward a brighter future.

The Don Coyhis and the Wellbriety movement have a "Healing Forest" metaphor (David Moore, 2010). The healing forest is our community and how well it serves in recovery. In this metaphor, there is a tree that is sick and dying. The soil it is in is toxic; it is not getting proper sunlight or nutrients. If you plant that tree in healthy soil and give it nutrients, care, and love, it will grow and thrive. We would never put that tree back in the same toxic environment we removed it from, yet we have done that with people for years. We have helped people build stability through residential treatment and other ways of early recovery. Then, we stick them right back in the environment they came from and wonder why so many people return to the old lifestyle. If we honestly had a healing forest (ROSC), our community would be better at recovery support and helping those we serve to continue to grow. I find it disappointing that we do with people what we would not do with plants.

As leaders, we must thoroughly comprehend the importance of establishing a comprehensive system of care within our communities. To effectively address the needs of a community, we must first grasp the true essence of what "community" entails. It goes beyond simply referring to a group of individuals living close to one another; community embodies a profound sense of camaraderie, inclusivity, and a shared sense of belonging. It surpasses the boundaries of physical location and permeates into the very fabric of fellowship, acceptance, and unity. By delving into the intricate dynamics of a community, we can better appreciate its complexities and intricacies, thereby enabling us to devise more effective strategies to fulfill its unique needs and foster its continued growth and well-being.

Recovery capital is an important part and foundation of the recovery process. The total resources a person has available to find and maintain recovery is their recovery capital. It includes a person's human and physical capital. Physical capital is the available resources to fulfill a person's needs, like healthcare, financial resources, clothing, food, shelter, and transportation. Human capital is a person's abilities, skills, and knowledge. The ability to navigate challenging situations connects to human capital. Human capital skills are interpersonal skills and a sense of meaning and purpose in life.

Family and social recovery capital play a crucial role in individuals' journey towards healing and rebuilding their lives. By cultivating deep and meaningful intimate relationships with family and friends, people in recovery establish a solid support system as a foundation for their recovery process. Supportive partners like spouses, romantic partners, or close friends are essential allies in this transformative journey. They serve as pillars of strength, providing encouragement, understanding, and empathy. These individuals offer emotional support and actively engage in activities and events that revolve around recovery.

Through their unwavering presence and commitment, supportive partners help create an environment conducive to positive change. They actively participate in recovery-related events, such as therapy sessions, support group meetings, and workshops, and find fun in recovery activities. It offers a steady source of motivation and reassurance. Their engagement in social interactions revolving around recovery helps individuals in healing forge new connections, strengthen existing ones, and regain a sense of belonging and purpose.

Furthermore, we cannot underestimate the significance of family in recovery capital. Close bonds forged within the familial unit provide stability, love, and acceptance - vital components for the healing process to thrive. Family members offer unique perspectives and insights, which can shed light on past patterns and dynamics that may have hindered recovery. They witness the changes and offer a constant reminder of the progress made, acting as a beacon of hope during challenging times. Ultimately, family and social recovery capital is integral to the recovery journey. The presence of supportive partners and nurturing family relationships provide individuals with an invaluable network of understanding and encouragement. Through these relationships, people in recovery can foster personal growth, build resilience, and embark on lasting transformation.

Community capital is a significant part of a ROSC.

Community capital includes attitudes, policies, and resources for helping people resolve barriers to enter and sustain the recovery process. Most communities have many resources that can help. One problem with the community capital is the lack of community communication to aid recovery. Leaders need to work at building better communication in a community. Cultural capital refers to a vast array of resources that profoundly resonate with an individual's cultural background, spiritual and religious beliefs. These resources encompass various elements, such as language, traditions, customs, and artistic expressions deeply rooted in a specific culture. **This rich tapestry of cultural capital plays a significant role in shaping one's identity and worldview.** It serves as a lens through which individuals perceive and interact with the world around them. As cultural beings, we are constantly navigating the intricacies of our cultural capital, drawing upon its wealth of knowledge, values, and symbols to navigate social interactions, make meaning of the world, and shape our personal beliefs and behaviors. This multifaceted and multidimensional concept of cultural capital encompasses the tangible and intangible aspects that create a symbiotic relationship between individuals and their cultural heritage, allowing them to maintain a solid connection to their roots while embracing the ever-evolving nature of culture and faith. By recognizing, appreciating, and harnessing the power of cultural capital, individuals can foster a profound sense of belonging, strengthen their cultural identities, and contribute to the vibrancy and diversity of our global society.

"This rich tapestry of cultural capital plays a significant role in shaping one's identity and worldview."

Recovery capital can improve coping strategies and enhance the quality of life in long-term recovery. Think of recovery capital as akin to having a well-endowed savings account that accumulates substantive resources over time. With each positive deposit made, your account becomes enriched, providing you with an extensive pool of assets to draw upon during times of crisis. This metaphorical reservoir of resilience grows in size and strength as you continue to invest in it, enabling you to navigate challenges and setbacks with greater poise and fortitude.

A ROSC has many elements that make it an entire system of care, a community of care. An essential element is person-centered care. Having a variety of pathways to support an individual improves the possibilities of sustained recovery. Allowing somebody choice and self-direction creates more motivation within each individual. As professionals in this field, we need to be better at understanding that recovery comes in many different forms. Our job is to understand the different options in our community so each individual can make choices that fit their personal beliefs.

Having family and other allies involved in the recovery process is extremely important for those we serve. **No one enters and remains in the recovery process by themselves.** Connecting the family of choice or origin with recovery and services improves the outcomes and the quality of life. Allies would include peer specialists, pastors, sponsors, and people along those lines who promote the system of care. An ally can be so crucial in building a level of safety and comfort. It helps individuals in recovery see that they are not alone. The entire support network, from families to allies, is part of that recovery experience. A healthy ROSC includes them and has options for them to be involved, creating a more cohesive path to recovery.

"No one enters and remains in the recovery process by themselves."

A ROSC looks at an individual plan of services for the individual's entire lifespan. Recovery is not a destination; it is a growing and changing journey. The services a person may need change as they continue moving forward. Continuity of care from systems anchored in the community over an individual's lifespan is vital to know and understand. Programs focus on strengths to build confidence and self-esteem that will span a lifetime.

Cultural aspects are a vital part of a ROSC. The behavioral health field strives for cultural humility. Some say cultural competence. I prefer the phrase cultural humility. Recovery systems are responsible for being culturally diverse, accepting, and caring. It's vital to be responsive to a person's belief systems to help support self-directed choice. Understanding the beautiful uniqueness of each individual in our community is a vital part of a recovery-oriented system. A healthy recovery community embraces diversity and lifts individuality while remaining a community. It takes people of diverse backgrounds and beliefs to build a healthy, flourishing community that supports individuals as human beings.

Recovery housing is vital when looking at recovery-oriented systems of care. Some houses and beds are healthy for people looking for recovery. There are fewer who have honest cultural humility and serve all populations. There is a significant scarcity of recovery housing options for individuals struggling with substance use. Having dedicated numerous years to working closely with the unhoused population, I have witnessed a glaring and sizable shortfall in providing transitional and permanent housing services tailored to these vulnerable groups' unique needs.

There continues to be a pervasive social stigma associated with the LGBTQ+ community, which serves as a barrier to acceptance and equality. This deep-seated bias affects individuals on a personal level and seeps into various aspects of their lives, including housing opportunities. One significant issue faced by the LGBTQ+ population is the lack of safe and inclusive housing options. Despite progress in recent years, many communities still struggle to provide an environment that wholeheartedly embraces this diverse group. Discrimination and prejudice persist, making it challenging for LGBTQ+ individuals to find suitable living spaces that respect their identities and ensure their safety and well-being. I worked for an agency that put an individual identified as female in a male residential program. She did not do well in that program. My objections did not help. We had a female program that she could have gone into. I could not even get support from the Missouri Department of Mental Health. I did reach out.

The absence of housing options specifically designed to cater to the unique needs and experiences of the LGBTQ+ community amplifies feelings of exclusion and vulnerability. Many LGBTQ+ individuals have encountered rejection and hostility from landlords or property managers due to their sexual orientation or gender identity. This rejection infringes upon their rights and creates a psychological toll of battling discrimination daily. Moreover, limited access to safe and affordable housing aggravates the problem. The high demand for LGBTQ+-friendly recovery housing surpasses the available supply. It creates additional hardships for individuals who may already face economic disparities and marginalization, further hindering their ability to secure stable and comfortable living arrangements.

Organizations and advocacy groups have been actively working towards fostering an inclusive environment and championing LGBTQ+ rights in recovery housing. Legislative measures have introduced ways to protect the rights of LGBTQ+ individuals seeking recovery housing, such as broader anti-discrimination laws that explicitly cover sexual orientation and gender identity. **Society must recognize and challenge the stigma perpetuating discrimination against the LGBTQ+ community.** By embracing diversity, promoting inclusivity, and ensuring equal treatment for all, we can create a society where everyone, irrespective of their sexual orientation or gender identity, has access to safe and welcoming recovery housing and treatment options that foster a sense of belonging and security.

"Society must recognize and challenge the stigma perpetuating discrimination against the LGBTQ+ community."

Components of a ROSC have adequate detox and treatment facilities with all forms and pathways to recovery. Harm reduction principles and programs can significantly reduce stigma and some of the trauma-activating issues we have in our communities. A ROSC includes treatment prevention, housing, family support, social services, criminal justice, faith culture, and everything about a community.

Recovery-oriented systems of care are all about support. Recovery support connects with emotional support, informational support, community support, and person-centered care.

Recovery happens in communities, and community-based resources have positively impacted recovery. Educating communities and creating continuity among support services recovery efforts and improved recovery outcomes help individuals live a more rewarding life. The reward is for the individual in recovery and the entire community. Communities that are ready and able to support a system of care include all of us. Leaders need to know their community's recovery-oriented systems of care to improve the quality of life and outcomes for our entire community.

Chapter Eight: Harm Reduction– Trauma-Informed Care, Unconditional Positive Regard, and Ethics

Harm reduction appears to be a new way to reach people. It's interesting how we continuously look for new ways to address issues in our profession. I remember when trauma-informed care became the buzzword for the helping profession. We also spoke about person-centered care for countless years and still do. But none of these are new. Harm reduction has existed for multiple years, even before Bill Wilson discussed it (Anonymous, 2020). Person-centered care has been around for 70-plus years. Carl Rogers made it famous, and we are still trying to understand its application (Unconditional Positive Regard, 2015). If you put everything together, trauma-informed care, person-centered care, and harm reduction are all part of the same modality. Yet for years, those of us in the helping professions have been focused on our field's moral and legal aspects thanks to a lack of education and the War on Drugs. Terminologies have changed, but the gist of "Do no Harm" should still be first and foremost in how we serve. We can do better.

Rogerian Theory by Carl Rogers, "person-centered care," discusses meeting people where they are. We've been looking at meeting them where we want them to be for innumerable years. Working in the field for years, I have seen many programs claim person-centered care and have strict rules that everybody must follow.... Think about that statement... A program in itself takes away from the ability to have person-centered care because it is programmatic care. Programs struggle because funding sources restrict the ability to have actual person-centered care. At the same time, as counselors and peer specialists, we could do more to truly meet somebody where they are without judgment and remember not to leave them there. Unconditional positive regard is the basic concept of accepting humans as humans and treating them as valuable. It has been a significant focus for the helping professions for years. People deserve better treatment and are considered valuable members of our world. We can do better. (Unconditional Positive Regard, 2015)

Trauma-informed care has a connection with do no harm, yet we tend to keep that focus on our language and the words we use (Trauma-Informed Care, 2023). Our language is vital in extending or reducing the stigma connected with behavioral health issues such as substance use disorder. Language and stigma can be vital to how we serve our communities and how our communities see those we serve. We have adopted this thinking as if it were one of our new children. We have embraced it as long as those we serve follow the path best for them, in our opinion.

We can delve into the complex and multifaceted concept of trauma, recognizing its profound impact on various issues directly affecting the individuals we serve. The Adverse Childhood Experiences (ACE) study provides valuable insights into the root causes behind specific behavioral patterns and actions exhibited by individuals who have experienced trauma. By exploring the findings and implications of this study, we can gain a deeper understanding of the connections between trauma and various aspects of an individual's life (CDC, 2020). We can do better.

You've noticed the common statement, "We can do better." It is because we can as we learn to do better, we should do better. Maya Angelou states it perfectly: "Do the best you can until you know better. Then when you know better, do better." (Caged Bird Legacy, 2023) We are at a point where we know better, so it's time to do better. It does not mean we replace everything that works successfully, but it does mean taking the knowledge we have so we can serve our communities better. One of the worst reasons someone can do something is because we've always done it that way. We can do better by pushing out the old moral models of punishment. **Harm reduction is not a new way of thinking but a new way of looking at what we already know.** We have had these theories and these models for years, but now we can look at them differently. The future of our field can grow and help more people.

> **"Harm reduction is not a new way of thinking but a new way of looking at what we already know."**

Harm reduction does not say destroy the system that is working; it says let's add layers on top of it. We can add a different way to look at those who struggle in a way that makes them feel cared for. Many studies discuss how a professional's relationship with the person they're serving can play a more significant role in an individual's progress than the modality used. It means we can build better relationships by stopping the stigma and the fear connected with the old way of seeing things. Abstinence is an excellent way for recovery but not the only way.

Let's look deeper at what we've been doing for years. We have been treating symptoms and ignoring the underlying issues like trauma, co-occurring, and many other things connected to social justice and equality or the lack thereof. Imagine this: If you will, a person breaks their arm, and they go to the doctor. The doctor gives them pain medication to treat the pain symptoms and then sends them on their way. The arm stays broken, and the pain will return. The underlying issue of the broken bone still exists. It is what we have done in treatment for countless years; we try to treat the symptom, the substance use disorder, before we treat the underlying issues. Doctors would not do this with a broken bone or other medical issues, but we have done it with behavioral health and substance use disorders for countless years. Harm reduction says let's look at the underlying issues as we address other goals that an individual may have. Imagine taking away the primary coping skill a person has. It opens the door to many other issues, including suicidal/homicidal ideations, violence, and other behavioral health issues.

We have spent a multitude of years punishing people for a trauma response. No one in our field would think we are causing harm by addressing symptoms that cause trouble in someone's life. But we have and do put people in situations that activate a trauma response and then punish them for it. Just think of how different it would be if those we serve genuinely felt cared for. Instead, they feel they need to hide urges or actual use because of the stigma and possible punishment. We have been missing part of the person we serve because we haven't made them comfortable. Many counselors say they have great relationships with those they serve, and I'm sure they do. But how deep is that relationship? Are they open and comfortable enough to tell you they want to continue using now or later in life?

"We have spent a multitude of years punishing people for a trauma response."

Most of our programs are funded and focused on abstinence as a goal rather than the quality of life. Our whole profession has been looking at abstinence as the end goal. Abstinence is a great goal; quality of life is a better goal. Thousands of people who stop using substances are miserable and have a low quality of life. It starts with us changing our views and helping those we serve to meet goals they feel are best for their future.

"Harm reduction focuses on raising the quality of life."

Harm reduction is a set of practical strategies and ideas to reduce the negative consequences of drug use. Harm

Reduction is also a movement for social justice built on a belief in and respect for the rights of people who use drugs (Harm Reduction, 2022). Keeping it simple, **"Harm reduction focuses on raising the quality of life."** The increase in quality of life is not for the person served alone but for the entire community. It includes better fathers, mothers, brothers, sisters, employees, and more. We are losing over 100,000 people a year to drug poisonings that end in death. Harm reduction services can save lives by being more accessible and emphasizing care and compassion toward those who use drugs. Harm reduction significantly prevents drug-related deaths and increases access to healthcare, social services, and treatment. These services decrease drug poisoning fatalities and life-threatening infections such as HIV and hepatitis.

Recovery is a simple but complex thing. Complex because it has many variables and factors, and each person is different. SAMHSA makes it simple with its definition.

"Recovery is a process of change through which individuals improve their health and wellness, live self-directed lives, and strive to reach their full potential."

(SAMHSA, SAMHSA's WORKING DEFINITION OF RECOVERY, 2012).

It is a process, not a destination. There are many different steps in a process. Some steps include improving health and wellness. People don't change because a counselor tells them to. They change when they tell themselves, IE. Self-directed. Finally, the people we serve are incredibly bright, and their potential is limitless when given a chance with care and love.

> SAMHSA defines harm reduction as a practical and transformative approach that incorporates community-driven public health strategies - including prevention, risk reduction, and health promotion - to empower PWUD and their families with the choice to live healthy, self-directed, and purpose-filled lives. Harm reduction centers on the lived and living experience of PWUD, especially those in underserved communities, on these strategies and the practices that flow from them. (SAMHSA, Harm Reduction Framework, 2023)

SAMHSA talks about Harm reduction services. These services can connect people with education, counseling, and referral to treatment for infectious diseases and substance use disorders. They help distribute opioid poisoning reversal medications like naloxone. We are lowering harms associated with drug use and related behaviors that increase the risk of infectious diseases like HIV and hepatitis. Reducing the stigma associated with substance use and co-occurring disorders is also essential. Much information supports a better way to serve people. Our communities can be stronger and more resilient when we add harm reduction principles to our daily practices (SAMHSA, Harm Reduction, 2023).

In SAMHSA's harm reduction framework, they talk about six pillars and twelve principles of harm reduction.

The first pillar discusses harm reduction principles and how people who use drugs (PWUD) and those with lived experience are the guides. The stigma connected with moral models and how people view PWUD makes this pillar difficult. Biases connected with these models build stigma and lower the likelihood of those voices being shared or heard. The lifestyle of people who use drugs is still looked down on and not given credit for the intelligence they have. It is important to note that people with lived experiences from their past have something to add to the conversation, but we need not forget those who still live the lifestyle. I have twenty-two years in recovery; my experience is different than that of somebody using it today. I want to hear their voice.

The second pillar talks about how we embrace people and value them. In the behavioral health field, you could say that this was very simply unconditional positive regard. The idea that someone has value regardless of their actions is vital and sometimes gets missed.

Our communities impacted by systematic harm connect to the third pillar. Programs and funding need to consider the culture of communities and how to serve them better. To better serve a community, first, you must allow that community to have a voice in what is needed—**many programs are designed with an outside-looking-in viewpoint that misses the authentic culture of a community**. Cultural humility, or as some say, cultural competence, is still a high priority in our world. It means that everybody's voice matters, that every person has value, and that the community they live in deserves to have a voice and services.

"Many programs are designed with an outside-looking-in viewpoint that misses the authentic culture of a community."

Pillar Four connects very well with Pillar Three as it discusses equity, human rights, and social justice. People place a very high value on good health, while it is generally regarded as unfair that certain groups within society do not have the same level of health resources. The injustice is perceived even more when there is an unequal distribution of resources like income, medical care, access to quality education, and healthy food supplies. Health inequalities are unjust and seem to be widespread across societies. There is little progress in implementing actual policies to reduce health inequalities. The policies made are made by those looking from the outside of the community.

Low-barrier programs are the basis for pillar five. Harm reduction services should have the lowest requirement for access. The idea that someone struggling in life and needing assistance is even willing or capable of jumping through significant hoops is unrealistic. The system has put so much emphasis on collecting data that we forget to meet people where they are and realize the trauma that can come from multiple assessments and questionnaires. That data is needed to show the quality of services and outcomes, but a harm reduction practice shows we can do it better. Policies connected to funding can harm rather than reduce harm. We must remove barriers that activate trauma and cause stress when people struggle to move forward.

"Change talk is where seeds are planted and may sprout later in life."

The sixth pillar is all about positive change in progress. For years, we have looked at recovery as a destination. Recovery is a process of change, not a destination but a process. Any step forward is essential to identify and provide affirmations. A step forward is simply admitting that a change may happen or something could be different to improve the quality of life. **Change talk is where seeds are**

planted and may sprout later in life. Quality of life needs to be the outcome we gauge rather than abstinence.

"Quality of life needs to be the outcome we gauge rather than abstinence."

Supporting principles start with respect and autonomy. Each individual has a right to make choices, and our job is to meet them where they are to help them raise their quality of life. Another principle of acceptance and hospitality is essential in harm reduction work. Programs should keep space open for people who are vulnerable or marginalized and emphasize how important a trusting relationship can be in helping motivate people. Having a place for someone not to feel so isolated and safe is enormous when motivating people to find personal success. Providing support is another area that can enhance and support an individual's positive change. Support needs to be non-judgmental, non-punitive, and compassionate, treating each individual as a human with empathy. Connecting with family is a principle that is imperative in adding a layer of safety. Families need to be part of services. Family of choice or family of origin does not matter as much as including them in safety practices, risk reduction, and drug poisoning responses.

An individual's family of choice or support network is vital in the recovery process, and the safety built by those individuals served. The need for many pathways is another pillar discussed by SAMHSA. It's essential to notice that everyone has a choice and is slightly different from the next. Acknowledging these differences in understanding different pathways to recovery can open doors to higher quality of life. One size does not fit; recovery comes in many different forms.

Structural racism and other forms of discrimination limit the voice of underserved communities. Harm reduction services understand the limitations and use wisdom and evidence from the community to build knowledge. The voice of those underserved communities can make a huge impact when we remove the bias and stigma surrounding them. Every community, every person deserves a voice in what programs and services are offered in their community. Cultivating these relationships is another principle that impacts harm reduction initiatives. The behavioral health field gets caught up in building a relationship with the individual and sometimes forgets the community. A relationship with the community is imperative, and serving the community and gaining an understanding of their viewpoints, beliefs, and goals. To build these relationships, harm reduction services need to assist, not direct—services based on what PWUD identifies as needs and goals. We do not want programs to promote services that they think are best for the person or community without the input of those in the community.

Safety is one of the supporting principles needed in a harm reduction approach. People do not move forward when they do not feel safe. It's essential to bring different communities that are marginalized and impacted to the table to build safe and meaningful relationships. It is the professional's responsibility to reach out and engage those communities. When these communities are engaged, one of the priorities should be listening. A powerful skill in the helping profession is keeping your mouth shut long enough to listen to what the person or the community says. The helping professions have had answers to many issues. Unfortunately, those answers met the needs of people's beliefs outside the community rather than the actual community or individuals themselves. Listening is the superpower that our world needs more of. The last principle SAMHSA discusses is working towards systems change. Many misunderstand harm reduction because they look at risk reduction as the foundation. Harm reduction is about changing the systems of inequality and injustice. We can include all voices. Everyone has a voice that should be heard and validated.

We can't underestimate the importance of safety regarding harm reduction practices. We've attached the idea of safety to the belief that abstinence was the only safe way to move forward. No debate not using substances can add a layer of safety to some people. Safety encompasses much more than using a substance. Many people with behavioral health issues use substances as a coping skill, and removing that level of safety for them adds danger. I have been a part of a harm reduction program in Missouri for veterans called Safe Haven for multiple years. Time and experience have shown that when those veterans felt safe, they were more likely to move forward.

It's important to realize that safety looks different for each individual. What appears safe for me in my life may not be the same for the person beside me. For most of my career, I have worked with the unhoused and put much effort into giving them a safe place to live. I have also encountered many issues assuming a safe place to live added safety. Many people I served felt safest in the camps or tents. Removing someone from a place they feel safe can be dangerous. Housing is vital. Emotional safety can look very different. When someone feels heard or their opinions matter, it adds comfort and safety. It's important to understand that an emotional, internal sense of comfort has immense power and provides safety to each individual.

As a clinician, I built the relationship needed to help people reach their personal goals. I've always worked in a person-centered program but learned years later that there is no such thing. Programs have claimed person-centered for years, but it is impossible because of the need for program rules that connect to funding. Many programs do a valiant job of trying to meet people where they are. The relationship

I worked to build is what creates a sense of safety between myself and the person I'm serving. Clinicians and peer specialists focus on building healthy relationships to improve people's ability to grow and move forward. Safety is the foundation of that relationship. The person served has to feel that they can be open and honest with every thought and process. **Stigma still plays a huge role in safety.** Internal and external beliefs make it hard for people to feel like they genuinely can be honest and open. Shame and guilt add to the internal stigma that reduces the feeling of safety. External stigmas are connected to blame and punishment. There's no way to connect stigmas and safeties in a successful program.

"Stigma still plays a huge role in safety."

Our legal system has made it hard to build safety. Punishment has been the foundation for many with substance use disorder and other behavioral health issues. After countless years, we can see that we will never arrest our way out of the crisis we are in. The War on Drugs has built an uneducated belief system and stigma, making it hard to build safety. Our prisons are full of people with a disease that gets treated as a crime rather than a health issue. Treating a person as a patient rather than a criminal adds safety. I do not want this misunderstood; many people deserve prison. My sentence was fair and just.

People spend years hiding who they are for fear of punishment and stigma. I have never met a person who could feel fear and safety simultaneously. We need to remove the fear of punishment to help add comfort and a willingness to move forward. The only way to remove the fear is to remove the punishment from our belief systems. Based on the moral model, our systems have added blame for years. The moral model has caused much of the stigma in our world today. There is no blame for other diseases, but substance use carries that stigma of moral judgment. We will never build safety until we change our belief in the moral model and moral judgment. Without safety, we will continue down our path and continue to incarcerate and criminalize instead of treating these medical issues.

Safe housing is one of the most significant issues we face in the recovery field today. There's a growing need for recovery houses that are healthy and good. The National Alliance for Recovery Residences (NARR) is raising the level and quality of houses for recovery. It's essential to have national standards to help build safety and have guidelines that will help protect those we serve. NARR-certified housing is making a massive difference across our country regarding healthier ways for people to continue with recovery support services (NARR, 2023). There is still more that we can do outside of the standard style of recovery houses in our communities.

"Safe housing is one of the most significant issues we face in the recovery field today."

The majority of recovery residences that are across the United States are connected to abstinence and still have a focus on punishment for those who use substances. These houses provide excellent services, but we're still lacking and missing a large portion of people who need services. Our housing models are not for somebody who still uses substances. Often, a person is put out of a house because of a return to use. The adage that high people activate others in the house trying to abstain is lacking. It does not lack validation; it lacks education. Our teams need training to help people when activated. If the only skill you teach is to remove the activating issue, you set them up to have struggles down the road. The education needed to build a safe environment is training staff to deal with somebody high. The safest place for an activating event is in a recovery residence or around professionals trained to help build resiliency. No matter what, people will run into intoxicated individuals and people who use substances for the rest of their lives. Proper education of the team working in those residences can make all the difference in understanding and using coping skills when activating events happen. Unfortunately, someone who has a return to use is labeled and punished.

There has been an emphasis on respite housing that helps in some ways and hurts others. It hurts because sending them to a respite house after returning to use is a punishment. Clients who have done well for weeks or months may struggle through a tough time and return to use for a short time. As a result, they have to pay the consequences of going to a respite house. The idea of sending someone to a respite house for a single event of returning to use is damaging and hurtful. The person who returned to use will hide it, possibly feel shame, and build a more extensive wall. The wall they build makes it hard for a counselor or a peer specialist to have an open, honest conversation or relationship. The wall built is not the client's fault; it is the result of the stigma connected to old-school beliefs. We can do better.

There needs to be more harm-reduction housing in our communities. Our programs and houses are abstinence-based, so they do not accept some harm reduction principles. The people we serve who try to work on their trauma and co-occurring behavioral health issues may feel unsafe in many of our communities' recovery houses. If a person doesn't have the goal of abstinence but still needs behavioral health services and housing, where do we send them? They will either need to hide part of who they are, which is not an honest relationship in a program, or go back to the toxic environment they came from. Recovery residences are far from being person-centered and following trauma-informed best practices. We need houses willing to meet people where they are with unconditional positive regard. Housing is one of the most vital parts of safety that we are missing in the recovery process for many people in our communities.

The Missouri Credentialing Board (MCB) has a Harm Reduction Credential (HRS) (MCB, 2021). The MCB has coordinated efforts with the International Certification & Reciprocity Consortium (IC&RC) to promote the HRS nationally (IC&RC, 2023). It is the first national harm reduction credential. The focus of the certification is to help professionals in the helping field be more open to helping those who do not fall into traditional treatment models. David Stoecker and I are the creators of the HRS training. Both have worked as counselors, peer specialists, and supervisors in behavioral health. The prime goal of this training and credential was to connect harm reduction principles and ethics. **We grow when professionals in this field understand how their code of ethics and the eight harm reduction principles from the National Coalition on Harm Reduction strengthen each other.** David and I put much effort into creating a training different than most expect. There is a discussion on the history of harm reduction and risk reduction techniques. Still, a significant part of this training focuses on how a professional can ethically use harm reduction. One prime point discussed is that you are unethical if you do not use certain harm-reduction practices in your daily work.

"We grow when professionals in this field understand how their code of ethics and the eight harm reduction principles from the National Coalition on Harm Reduction strengthen each other."

Key points for the HRS national credential are listed below.

- Increase knowledge around Harm Reduction and its use in recovery processes.
- Apply skills within a harm reduction framework to current practice
- Feel comfortable having conversations around harm reduction with clients and the community
- Identify obstacles in applying harm reduction and develop strategies to overcome these obstacles
- Learn to engage people who are continuing to use substances in harm-reduction recovery practices
- Build the foundation for clinical and non-clinical communication around harm reduction strategies

The National Coalition of Harm Reduction has eight foundational principles.

1. Accepts, for better or worse, that licit and illicit drug use is part of our world and chooses to work to minimize its harmful effects rather than simply ignore or condemn them

2. Understands drug use as a complex, multi-faceted phenomenon that encompasses a continuum of behaviors from severe use to total abstinence and acknowledges that some ways of using drugs are clearly safer than others

3. Establishes quality of individual and community life and well-being — not necessarily cessation of all drug use — as the criteria for successful interventions and policies

4. Calls for the non-judgmental, non-coercive provision of services and resources to people who use drugs and the communities in which they live in order to assist them in reducing attendant harm

5. Ensures that people who use drugs and those with a history of drug use routinely have a real voice in the creation of programs and policies designed to serve them

6. Affirms people who use drugs (PWUD) themselves as the primary agents of reducing the harms of their drug use and seeks to empower PWUD to share information and support each other in strategies that meet their actual conditions of use

7. Recognizes that the realities of poverty, class, racism, social isolation, past trauma, sex-based discrimination, and other social inequalities affect both people's vulnerability to and capacity for effectively dealing with drug-related harm

8. Does not attempt to minimize or ignore the real and tragic harm and danger that can be associated with illicit drug use

(PRINCIPLES OF HARM REDUCTION, 2020)

Read each principle and process the meanings. While you process the meanings of each principle, connect them with your code of ethics. After many trainings, David and I have discovered that participants realize ethics and harm reduction principles strengthen each other. After completing this training, you will see and understand the importance of breaking stigmas connected to harm reduction. After the three-day training, you will have more skills and tools for applying harm reduction practices ethically in the helping profession.

"The framework of harm reduction can apply to any clinical practice."

Harm reduction is a philosophy that encourages people to make choices to avoid or reduce harm. Harm reduction discusses drug use and risky behaviors like gambling or unsafe sex. **The framework of harm reduction can apply to any clinical practice.** It is a way of thinking about the client's needs and goals, the service environment, and how to meet them with a non-judgemental stance. Harm reduction is not just about substances but also includes harm reduction in other areas, such as sexual and mental health. When working with clients who continue to use substances, it is essential to understand why they are using them. It will help you understand what motivates them and how they may respond differently to different strategies. When working with clients who have complex needs, it is essential to develop a relationship with them so that you can work together on their recovery journey. You may need to identify obstacles within yourself or your environment before applying harm-reduction strategies effectively. You can overcome these obstacles and support your clients through their recovery process by understanding them better.

Many people feel uncomfortable discussing harm reduction with their clients and the community. They may be worried about being perceived as encouraging drug use or that they will make clients feel guilty or ashamed for their actions. However, harm reduction can be an effective way to help clients make positive lifestyle changes and reduce risks associated with drug use. It is essential to feel comfortable having these conversations so you can provide quality care. There is much education needed when it comes to talking about harm reduction. It is crucial to help people understand that the old way of looking at recovery can be damaging. The more comfortable you are talking about harm reduction, the more likely the people you serve will be comfortable. Conversations with some level of comfort build better relationships with those we serve. Comfort and safety are connected and vital to a good relationship.

The main obstacle to harm reduction is the stigma surrounding substance use. Many people believe that if you use drugs, you are somehow less of a person than someone who does not. This stigma can lead to discrimination against drug users in social settings, employment opportunities, and housing options. To overcome this obstacle, we must first recognize that no one deserves to be discriminated against based on drug use. Next, we need to educate others about the benefits of harm reduction and encourage them to support those who struggle by welcoming them into social environments and seeking treatment when needed or requested.

Learn to engage people who are continuing to use substances in harm-reduction discussions. We can better meet people where they are with acceptance and care. Trauma-informed care tells us that the words we use can hurt or heal. Learning how to talk to those who still use substances in a way that does not activate a trauma or behavioral health response can be crucial. The people we serve are very bright and intelligent. How we engage these people can impact how well somebody will feel cared for. Engaging these bright individuals with bias or stigma will be seen and felt by those you are trying to help. Unconditional positive regard is about treating each individual as a valued member of society and as a human being. Engaging people with respect and dignity is essential in a harm-reduction approach.

The main idea behind the harm reduction credential

through the Missouri credentialing board is to set a foundation for better practices. Communication between clinical and non-clinical can cause trouble in many instances. The training for the harm reduction credential is about setting a foundation for better practices. I use the phrase better practices instead of best practices because we are still learning so much about how to serve people and treat them with respect. There is no best practice; rather, we are simply learning to do better.

Harm reduction is more than a clinical or non-clinical practice; it is a way of life. Our world is in chaos and struggling to treat people with respect. In simplistic terms, harm reduction means that each individual deserves respect and love. People who may not fall into the same categories of abstinence or meeting the treatment goals that society has set still deserve respect. In my years of teaching professionals to improve behavioral health practices, I have learned that we harm as often as we avoid harm. I do not believe the intention is to harm, but when we genuinely do not meet people where they are and accept them still as humans, we harm. We can do better, learn more, and become more accepting and less critical. Harm reduction is the human approach to dignity and respect, creating a sense of safety and love. (Vick, 2023)

"Harm reduction is more than a clinical or non-clinical practice; it is a way of life."

Chapter Nine: A Willingness to Learn

Willingness to learn is a critical skill that helps us move forward in life, personally and professionally. Being open to new experiences, skills, and information improves our abilities and enjoyment. We start learning early, but being open to continued learning can help us form skills as adults. It shows adaptability to a changing world and circumstances. It helps us develop essential skills like time management, communication, and emotional intelligence. Being willing to learn is an essential skill for leadership growth. It is crucial to train and develop your skills. Learning about your business, community, and profession would be best. Your tools and procedures will change with time, even if you stay in the same job. Being open helps you learn new working methods and could help you do your job better. Nobody comes into a job already knowing everything. Everyone must learn the process, discover their way around the company, and even learn the basics.

"I Reserve The Right To Be Wrong."

The ability and willingness to learn will help you build competence quickly. It helps you develop better techniques and take on important information. Hiring people who can demonstrate a willingness to learn is essential. It doesn't mean we are looking for academic excellence. Having a commitment to learning is an attitude that anyone can have. Being willing to develop your skills and further your knowledge is crucial in the workplace. It appears simple when hiring, but you must keep the same attitude as a leader. I return to my statement, **"I Reserve The Right To Be Wrong."** As a leader, I have made many mistakes. The biggest mistake has been thinking I'm good and I know everything about a situation.

Anyone who has gained a certification/qualification is willing and able to learn. It is particularly true if you've pursued higher education or gained vocational certifications. A lack of qualifications doesn't mean someone lacks the willingness to learn. Think about your time in school and the subjects you enjoyed. For those classes, you might seek out more information and knowledge. You may do extra reading on a topic if it sparks your interest. Getting involved in extra-curricular activities demonstrates a willingness to learn and develop new skills.

The connection between willingness and learning is being curious. We might ask questions like 'Why do we do that?' or 'How do I solve that problem?'. **Good leaders turn this curiosity into learning.** Embracing your team's curiosity is vital in motivating their effort.

"Good leaders turn this curiosity into learning."

Ask your team where they want to be in the future. Find out what job they would like to be doing. Help them visualize what they want, both short-term and long-term. It helps motivate people to learn skills to achieve goals. It's never more accessible or more enjoyable to learn than when the subject is something close to your heart. When you're lucky to work at doing something you love or care passionately about, learning will likely come naturally.

I have always tried to excel at anything and everything I've done. This drive has always helped me to study, learn, and find ways to help me grow. I have always been one of those people who wants to know why and how everything works. I have spent years asking why and how because I wanted to learn. With each step in my career ladder, I have come up against new challenges and embraced them with the willingness and desire to improve.

The desire to succeed is common in many people in our world. Many people desire status titles or more money. They may work hard to achieve these goals. It's great to have a desire to try to move forward and achieve more. But desire only takes you so far if you're unwilling to be open-minded and learn. Willingness is the factor that I think many people miss. A person may want to move forward and make more money but are unwilling to do the extra work that may change their viewpoint. I came into the behavioral health field thinking I knew what recovery looked like. I had a desire to help the person across the desk meet the goals that I thought were best for their life so they could be active, productive members of society.

There are things wrong with the statement I just made. I had to desire to help somebody do what I thought was best is the error in that statement. I am willing to identify that people enter recovery and move forward better when it is their goal, not mine. I also need to point out that everybody is an active member of society. Just because someone struggles does not mean they are not valuable or productive. My willingness to learn has grown because I stay open-minded to new ideas and ways to serve. I'm good at what I do, but know I can still learn. I love the statement by Maya Angelou, "Do the best you can until you know better, then when you know better, do better." (Caged Bird Legacy, 2023) I have taken this to heart, meaning do the best I can until I learn better. I then need to do the best I can until I learn better and then do better. Then, I need to do the best I can until I learn better so I can do better. As you notice, from the multiple sentences, it is a pattern for me. I'm willing to do my best, believing I can improve as I learn. That phrase keeps on rotating and rotating and rotating in my mind and heart. Do the best I can until I learn better, then take that better and do the best I can until I learn better, then do the best I can. All this is not possible if I'm not willing to learn, not willing to grow. **Desire is not enough. You have to be willing to learn, open your mind, and accept that there are different ways and knowledge than what we possess now.**

"Desire is not enough. You have to be willing to learn, open your mind, and accept that there are different ways and knowledge than what we possess now."

My intentions with this chapter are to point out that you, as a leader, and those on your team need to be willing to learn. It would be best to be open-minded to allow your team's opinions to impact your daily work. My time as a leader has proven that I need to listen to the team because I don't know everything. I do not have to use every idea the team comes up with, but I have to be open to it. If I do not show the willingness and openness to listen to my team and use some of their ideas, they will stop talking and stop providing ideas. Your team may become quiet if you're unwilling to listen to them and learn different viewpoints. A quiet team is not a team of leaders but of followers. I want a team full of leaders. There is more than one way to achieve almost every goal. Be open to listening to your team and accepting different pathways. It would help if you also were not afraid of mistakes. Mistakes are how we learn and how we grow. I have learned more in my career from errors in my thinking than from the successes of my actions. A willingness to learn makes a mistake a benefit rather than an error. I use each learning lesson as a stepping stone rather than a stumbling block.

Chapter Ten: Why It All Matters And How It All Comes Together

> " A PLAN NOT WRITTEN DOWN IS JUST A WISH "

I've spent numerous years as a leader on multiple teams. Years ago, I learned how to communicate with employees as a foreman on a construction crew. I yelled and directed actions. After I moved to the behavioral health field, I learned that communicating with carpenters was very different from communicating with treatment teams. I started to think about the feelings of my employees more. As I thought about the feelings of each person working with me, I discovered that they were part of a team, not employees.

The simple way we say things has an impact on how people feel. Think about how you talk to and about your team. My skills as a leader had to adapt and evolve and grow.

Over the years, I have received many blessings from working with great people. People have told me I built some of the best teams anybody has ever worked on. I have always stated that the entire team made the team great. There is also the understanding that I set a foundation that made it easier for the team to excel.

Why does the team matter so much in the behavioral health field in the recovery world? For those that work in this field, it's clear. **A healthy team creates a better program with better outcomes.** I have never liked the idea of money being the motivating factor for a program. But the simple fact is you have to keep the doors open so you can help the next person who walks in. Outcomes and funding are connected, so a healthy team is vital. The team approach increases positive outcomes. With better outcomes, you have better funding and more ability to serve our community. A group of people who feel unified as a team provides better services because they feel better about their daily routine. The positive mental health of each individual on a team is critical.

"Desire is not enough. You have to be willing to learn,"

Life happens, and people struggle, especially in the

behavioral health field. Expectations are high, and resources are low, and this leads to burnout and unhealthy teams. Having a good team promotes an environment of support and care that will lower stressors and barriers to positive mental health. We meet people at some of the lowest points in their lives when they're unhappy and struggling. It can be easy to take on the feel or transference from them. We may carry a load that isn't ours to carry. We carry it because that is why we got into this profession, to help. Having a supportive team helps distribute some of that load. It also helps us reflect with each other on how much of that load is valid. When team members have a bad day, they know others will not think less of or treat them differently but will support and lift them through their struggles. Bad teams point out bad days and focus on the struggle. I've been part of teams like this and seen the damage they can do. It has been motivational to me to be a part of teams that support each other. We should never create extra work for a team member if we can avoid it. Many team members are givers, and having a team member who takes advantage of that is unhealthy.

It all starts to come together when you focus on your team's mental health more than your program's outcomes. Many leaders have focused on outcomes first and then their team's health. A simple fact is that a healthy team will have better outcomes. My experience from the places I have ever worked has taught me to focus on the team first. Anyone who has flown has heard the flight attendant say that if the oxygen mask drops, put it on yourself first before you help somebody else. It is the same with our teams; focus on them first. We need to focus on what makes us feel healthy and productive. I can serve and be a better team member when I feel healthier. It is an issue because we tell clients and people to focus on themselves. Then, we focus on outcomes before we focus on those that help facilitate the outcomes. I will restate that **healthy teams help create better outcomes.**

"Healthy teams help create better outcomes."

Professionals in this field are role models. The people we serve are watching our movements and attitudes. We consistently teach healthy boundaries, self-care, and wellness. Teaching and being an example are two different things. The people we serve are very bright and intelligent. Clients see what we do and hear what we say. If those don't line up, the professional loses credibility with a client they're trying to serve. Role models aren't perfect, but they exhibit healthy ways of dealing with struggles.

You are in this field to help. If you have taken the time to read this book (thank you), you are interested in learning different ways to be an effective leader. I want to focus on the word effective for a minute. My definition of effective leaders may be a little different than others. Effective means that the team sees and feels that your leadership is an asset to them. The word "feels" is essential when discussing effectiveness because how your team feels will directly impact how they function. Effective leaders promote healthy feelings within a team that improves functions and outcomes.

I have seen how this works regarding how the team feels. I have also seen the results of the clients served and how they talked about how those programs were different from other programs they have been in. If you have a program where the team feels valued and heard, you will also have a program that promotes that feeling within the client served. Multiple studies have talked about how meaningful the relationship is rather than the modality used within the counseling relationship. The same is true for a team's relationship, regardless of team members' level or title. We use unconditional positive regard with clients and must use it with each other. **Unconditional positive regard should be a way of life, not just something we say in our program**. The healthier the team you have, the healthier the program you have. If you have a healthier program, you have better outcomes; with better outcomes, there are more funding possibilities. I never want all this to be about money, but it does play a significant role in our programs. Your program will receive better funding if you foster a healthy team approach.

"Unconditional positive regard should be a way of life, not just something we say in our program."

Leadership is a privilege. You can teach leadership skills, but attitude and beliefs are more challenging to inspire. Unfortunately, many leaders think they need to be perfect and know everything. We can be better at lifting leaders who genuinely want to serve and teaching those who want to be the boss. If you want to be the boss, you may not have gotten much out of this book. My goal as a leader is to serve, support, lift, and help others meet their goals. There were times when my actions did not match my current beliefs. I would have fired myself more than likely if I were my boss years ago. Thankfully, I have grown and been part of some fantastic teams and learned how to support our community and team better. You can make a change in our world. It doesn't come from shouting; look at what I've done. It comes from shouting; look at what our team has done or what WE have done.

Be a servant leader with an authentic style; you can change many things in our field. I will forever be a servant to the teams I'm a part of, even after years of separation. You have the ability; you need to focus on yourself first, then your team, clients, and community.

Your focus for yourself must be on humility and a willingness to learn.

Your focus for the team needs to be connected to support and understanding.

Your focus on the team will improve outcomes and our community!

Please remember that you are a star, and you matter.

We Are Better Together.

Additional Information - Recovery Consulting

Over the past decade, I have been approached by numerous professionals and programs seeking assistance. I have come to find that Missouri's recovery and treatment community embodies a remarkable openness to learning and growth. It has been incredibly fulfilling for me to train countless professionals, equipping them with the tools they need to support better those facing challenges. Central to the core of my training and mentoring philosophy is instilling crucial skills in self-care and fostering effective teamwork. In our field, self-care often takes a backseat, leading to a decline in our ability to work cohesively as a team when we encounter personal struggles. Recognizing that these struggles extend beyond our clients, encompassing individuals, teams, and programs, is essential. My passion lies in the mentor role, as I derive great satisfaction from guiding others along their professional journeys.

Recovery Consulting emerged from a deeply rooted conviction that my potential for impact could be amplified by dedicating myself to education, training, and mentorship. Encouraged by numerous team members who recognized my abilities, I embarked on a journey to establish a company and author a book. And now, behold, this very book exists: Recovery Leadership. Likewise, the company is none other than Recovery Consulting LLC. Reflecting upon my transition to this new phase, an undeniable sense of peculiarity washes over me. No longer situated within the confines of a physical office or interacting with colleagues daily, the experience of working from my home office is an intriguing contrast. It necessitates cultivating diverse skills and knowledge as I strive toward self-sufficiency and adaptability.

As the executive director of past organizations, I have faced the crucial task of cultivating widespread public awareness for my programs. As a founder, I engage in many similar activities. However, my focus has recently shifted towards articulating and highlighting my contributions and expertise rather than solely emphasizing my team's collective achievements and abilities. Historically, I have excelled at championing the team's qualities and extolling the virtues of our programs. My belief in these aspects has remained unwavering over time. Nevertheless, I am currently discovering that I possess the capability to also believe in the services provided by Recovery Consulting, which I offer. (Vick, Recovery Consulting, 2023)

I wanted to add some statements I received when I started this venture. Many of my past team members added recommendations on Google.

Larry moved on from Benilde Hall and now does great things at a program in Kansas. He has been a great person and one of the brightest people I know. Larry posted:

> I had the honor and pleasure of working with Ken Vick for over two years. I was a counselor at Benilde Hall, a treatment facility serving homeless men suffering from co-occurring substance use disorders and mental health issues. Ken was the executive director during the span of my employment. However, he was much more than the director. He was a mentor and a priceless

source of knowledge regarding the disease of addiction and the professional ethics involved with addiction counseling. In fact, I still call Ken to this day when I have a complicated ethical dilemma.

In addition, Ken is one of the most amazing addiction counselors I have ever witnessed. His ability to integrate his knowledge and skills with his person-centered style of motivational interviewing yields comparable results. Of equal importance, Ken's knowledge of the disease of addiction is equaled by his knowledge of what life in recovery truly looks like, understanding that recovery is not an event but a process striving to reach one's full potential that lasts for life. I would highly recommend Mr. Vick to anyone wishing to supplement their resources with expert knowledge and guidance. (Vick, Recovery Consulting, 2023)

I had the privilege of first encountering Larry when he joined Benilde Hall for his practicum classes. When he joined our team, it became clear to Erin Fraser, the clinical director of Benilde Hall, and myself that Larry possessed extraordinary talent and dedication. It was a unanimous decision that Larry should continue his journey with us. For more than two years, Larry contributed significantly to the growth and success of Benilde Hall. His commitment and passion were unparalleled, inspiring his colleagues and the individuals we served. It was evident that he possessed the qualities of a natural leader. Although Larry eventually moved on to pursue opportunities in a different program, our connection remains strong. I am grateful for the continued contact and the opportunity to witness the remarkable accomplishments he has achieved. Larry's impact on our team left a lasting impression, and he is cherished.

We have all experienced the profound influence of at least one remarkable teacher or professor who has left an indelible mark on our lives. Mary Vorsten, a distinguished educator, was a professor at Metropolitan Community College in Kansas City, Missouri. Her dedication and expertise have enriched my academic journey and offered me countless blessings and opportunities. Moreover, Mary's steadfast commitment to nurturing her students' growth is evident. She often recommends them for internships within my programs, providing valuable hands-on experiences essential to their professional development. Shiloh was one of those. He posted:

> Recovery Consulting is an organization
> passionate about helping others to empower
> those in our community to work on their

substance use disorders, housing issues, and tackling life issues.

Ken Vick is here to help enable others and inspire all to lead their teams, educate themselves on pressing issues, and to equip those in the field to be their best so that they may encourage clients and coworkers! In my opinion, everyone can grow by contacting Recovery Consulting and Ken Vick! (Vick, Recovery Consulting, 2023)

Shiloh came to Benilde Hall for our meeting about an article related to his ongoing classes. Once we had discussed his paper's specific requirements and objectives, our conversation organically veered toward the broader topic of recovery and other issues central to our program and beliefs. During our exchange, Shiloh expressed his earnest desire to undertake his practicum here once his classes commenced. This decision worked well for Benilde and the individuals benefitting from its services. It was evident that Shiloh approached our conversation with an appetite for knowledge, absorbing every fragment of information he could and incorporating it into his study. Shiloh has become a dedicated full-time counselor at an esteemed program in Kansas City, a testament to his unwavering commitment and the tremendous progress he has made in his professional journey.

I am genuinely interested in delving into the experiences I've had with my previous team members and exploring the rich tapestry of stories they have shared with me. The teams I've had the privilege of being a part of fostered a strong camaraderie as we provided unwavering support to one another. Even though we have gone our separate ways, we have maintained regular contact, allowing us to strengthen the bonds that form our unique community continually. Reflecting on my journey, I will delve deep into teamwork and its immense impact. Recovery Consulting aims to help other leaders and programs gain what I have been a part of. I am incredibly fortunate to have collaborated with exceptional individuals who have graced my teams. Whether through the written word or extensive spoken discussions, I am confident I could passionately articulate the significance of a unified team.

Moreover, these conversations would serve as a platform to showcase the qualities possessed by each team member. However, I must acknowledge that I may have inadvertently overlooked other valuable contributions in my focus on the quotes attributed to Larry and Shiloh. I genuinely do not wish for anyone to feel excluded or left behind. The messages conveyed by all team members have deeply resonated with me and beautifully embody the principles that I tirelessly strive to promote through my work in Recovery Consulting.

I would be remiss if I did not take the opportunity to delve into the details surrounding the remarkable individuals known as Jenna and Hannah. Jenna embarked on her journey with me more than five years ago, assuming the peer specialist role. Meanwhile, Hannah emerged onto the scene around the same time, fresh out of college and eager to make a difference as a substance use counselor. Together, the three of us have cultivated a unique synergy and collaborative spirit that has the potential to enhance various programs significantly. It is particularly relevant when we consider the invaluable contributions that counselors, peer specialists, and supervisors can make when they join forces.

As mentioned, it is unfortunate that many supervisors lack a solid understanding of effectively harnessing a peer specialist's potential. However, through my professional certifications as a peer specialist, clinician, and supervisor, we have created a dynamic that serves our community and sets an example for others. Jenna and Hannah have forged a remarkable working relationship that sparks a synergistic effect whenever they join forces to assist those in need. Their collaboration seamlessly blends the worlds of peer services and clinical expertise to reinforce each other and ultimately lead to positive outcomes. It is worth noting that achieving such unity within a team can prove challenging for many. Frequently, this difficulty stems from a lack of understanding regarding each team member's specific role. Thankfully, the three of us have successfully navigated these potential pitfalls, primarily due to our shared humility and unwavering focus on the ultimate objective: to benefit the individuals we serve. Our work is not about personal ego but rather the sincere desire to make a positive impact on those who rely on our support.

These statements shed light on the strong connection between a cohesive team and positive outcomes within our profession. We must strengthen our support for one another while also emphasizing the importance of supervisors providing better assistance to the team. Extensive research has consistently shown that when teams receive sufficient support and work together harmoniously, they are far more likely to produce favorable results and effectively serve the community. Our communities rightfully deserve more streamlined programs with outstanding outcomes. Better communities are why I founded Recovery Consulting - intending to help programs achieve this level of comprehension and success.

We must strive to overcome the barriers that divide us, even within our programs. Collaboration within our programs from team to team is lacking in many companies. Too many of our programs have poor communication with other programs. We can make a significant impact by leveraging the available resources within our community. Achieving this relies on our collective teamwork, ensuring that we effectively serve the individuals we are devoted to helping and maximizing the use of allocated funds. Unfortunately, numerous programs operate inefficiently in spending and using public tax dollars. However, we possess the power to rectify this situation. Throughout the years, I have dedicated myself to budget management, securing grants, and other financial responsibilities, all while developing strategies to enhance economic viability and ensure the sustainability of programs. Recovery Consulting can help create a noteworthy difference if we collaborate and put aside personal egos to serve our community.

References

Anonymous, A. (2020). *Alcoholics Anonymous*. Retrieved from Alcoholics Anonymous: https://www.aa.org/

Caged Bird Legacy, L. (2023). *Maya Angelou*. Retrieved from Caged Bird Legacy, LLC.: https://www.mayaangelou.com/

CDC. (2020). *About the CDC-Kaiser ACE Study*. Retrieved from CDC: https://www.cdc.gov/violenceprevention/aces/about.html

Claremont Lincoln Univesity. (2023). *Claremont Lincoln Univesity*. Retrieved from Claremont Lincoln Univesity: https://www.claremontlincoln.edu/?utm_source=gmb&utm_medium=organic

David Moore, P. (2010). *The Healing Forest Environmental Prevention Process: Community Effectiveness through Coalition Program Evaluation* . White Bison, Inc . Retrieved from Wellbriety: https://wellbrietymovement.com/

Greenleaf, R. K. (2020). Retrieved from Robert K. Greenleaf Center For Servant Leadership: https://www.greenleaf.org/what-is-servant-leadership/

Harm Reduction. (2022). Retrieved from SAMHSA: https://www.samhsa.gov/find-help/harm-reduction

IC&RC. (2023). *IC&RC INTERNATIONAL CERTIFICATION & RECIPROCITY*

CONSORTIUM. Retrieved from IC&RC INTERNATIONAL CERTIFICATION & RECIPROCITY CONSORTIUM: https://internationalcredentialing.org/

MCB. (2021). *Missouri Credentialing Board*. Retrieved from MissouriCB: https://missouricb.com/

NARR. (2023). *NARR*. Retrieved from National Alliance for Recovery Residences: https://narronline.org/

PRINCIPLES OF HARM REDUCTION. (2020). Retrieved from harmreduction.org: https://harmreduction.org/about-us/principles-of-harm-reduction/

SAMHSA. (2012). *SAMHSA's WORKING DEFINITION OF RECOVERY*. Retrieved from SAMHSA: https://store.samhsa.gov/sites/default/files/d7/priv/pep12-recdef.pdf

SAMHSA. (2017). TAP 21 Addiction Counseling Competencies. Rockville, MD.

SAMHSA. (2023, 4 24). *Harm Reduction*. Retrieved from SAMHSA: https://www.samhsa.gov/find-help/harm-reduction

SAMHSA. (2023). *Harm Reduction Framework*. SAMHSA.

Sinek, S. (2023). *Find Your Why*. Retrieved from The Optimism Library: https://simonsinek.com/books/find-your-why/

Trauma-Informed Care. (2023). Retrieved from Aces Aware: https://www.acesaware.org/ace-fundamentals/principles-of-trauma-informed-care/

Unconditional Positive Regard. (2015). Retrieved from
   Good Therapy:
   https://www.goodtherapy.org/blog/psychpedia/unco
   nditional-positive-regard

Vick, K. (2023, July 19). Harm Reduction. Kansas City,
   Missouri, United States of America.

Vick, K. (2023, July 1). *Recovery Consulting.* Retrieved
   from Recovery Consulting:
   https://www.recoveryconsulting.net/